Contents

Who was Claude Monet?

Claude Monet was a French artist. He was one of the **Impressionists**. This group of painters tried to show how light changed through the day in their paintings.

Claude painted the same **scene** many times to show the change of light. This painting shows clouds **reflected** in the lily pond in his garden.

Early years

Claude Oscar Monet was born in Paris, France, on 14 November 1840. His family soon moved to the **port** of Le Havre. Claude liked being near the sea.

Claude loved the way light showed on water. This drawing shows the coast near Le Havre. Claude drew the picture when he was 24 years old.

Schoolboy success

Claude did not like school. He made clever drawings of his classmates. A local painter called Eugène Boudin saw these drawings. He wanted Claude to become a painter.

Claude could pick out the important bits to draw. He was 16 years old when he made this funny drawing of a young man dressed in stylish clothes.

Making friends

In 1861 Claude joined the army but became ill after a year. His family gave him some money to become a painter. Claude moved to Paris when he was 22 years old.

Claude became close friends with other young artists in Paris. They often painted together. Claude painted this **scene** on a trip to the countryside near Paris.

Living in London

In 1870 Claude married Camille Doncieux. France was at war with Germany. Paris was dangerous so Claude and his wife moved to London. This is a picture of how London looked then.

Claude and his wife lived for a while in London. Claude saw many paintings by English artists. He painted the River Thames many times while he was in London.

Discovering light

In 1871 Claude moved to Argenteuil, a small town near Paris. He built a floating **studio** to **study** how light affects water. This is a picture of Claude painting in his studio.

Claude liked to paint outside in every season. This painting shows a street in Argenteuil in the winter. He painted it in 1875.

Impressionism

Claude and his friends painted quickly. Most **galleries** thought their paintings looked messy. In 1874 the group **exhibited** their own paintings. The exhibition was in a building in this street.

The group became known as the
Impressionists. The name came
from the title of this painting by
Claude called *Impression, Sunrise*.
It shows a harbour just after **dawn**.

Two families

Claude and his family moved to a town called Vétheuil. They moved in with their friend Alice Hoschede and her children. Claude now had to look after two families and eight children.

Claude began painting around his new home in Vétheuil. He used quick **strokes** of the brush to show light and shape.

Giverny

In 1879 Claude's wife Camille died. In 1883 Claude and the two families moved to Giverny, near Paris. He loved his new garden. He also painted in the countryside.

Claude worked quickly. He began painting the same **scenes** over and over. This painting tells us about the houses, fields, and even the weather in one afternoon.

Painting trips

Claude spent many months away from home each year during the 1880s. He travelled around France and painted many **landscapes**. He worked in all sorts of weather.

This painting shows the seashore in the south of France. Claude used quick **brushwork**. We can almost feel the wind blowing through the trees and across the sea.

Series paintings

Claude kept painting the same **scenes** at different times. Together these pictures are known as his **series paintings**. He painted this **cathedral** at Rouen many times.

Claude loved to paint the front of Rouen Cathedral. It is almost hidden by mist in this picture. Other paintings show it in bright sunshine.

Travels

Claude made his
last painting trips
when he was
over 60 years old.
He went to Spain,
Holland, England,
and Italy. This
is a picture of
Claude and Alice
in Venice, Italy.

Claude loved the buildings in Venice.
They rise straight out of the water.
This painting shows a beautiful palace
reflected in the water.

Water lilies

Claude spent his last years at home in Giverny. He still thought about light and shape. He died on 5 December 1926. He was 86 years old.

Many of Claude's last works were huge paintings of water lilies. In this painting it is hard to tell where the lilies end and their **reflections** begin.

Timeline

1840   Claude Monet is born in Paris on 14 November, but soon moves
            to Le Havre.

1857   Claude meets the painter Eugène Boudin.

1862   Claude moves to Paris to become a painter.

1865–66   Claude has paintings shown to the public in Paris.

1870   Claude marries Camille Doncieux and lives in London.

1870–71   War between France and Germany.

1871   Claude moves to a new house in Argenteuil.

1874   Claude helps set up the first **exhibition** by the **Impressionists**.

1879   Camille dies. The artist Paul Klee is born in Switzerland.

1883   Claude moves to Giverny.

1893   Claude begins work on building a pond in the garden
            at Giverny.

1909   First public showing of Claude's water lily paintings.

1912   Claude develops an eye illness which slows his painting.

1926   Claude Monet dies on 5 December.

Glossary

brushwork marks left by an artist's paint brush

cathedral large church

dawn when it starts to get light in the morning

exhibit display works of art

gallery place where works of art are shown and sold

Impressionists group of artists who painted freely, showing light and movement

landscape painting of the countryside

port city on the edge of the ocean

reflect give a second picture of something, as with a mirror

scene place or area

series paintings many paintings of the same subject but painted at different times

stroke mark made by one movement of the brush

studio special room or building where an artist works

study to learn about a subject

More books to read

Masterpieces: Monet, Shelly Swanson Sateren (Franklin Watts, 2004)

The Children's Book of Art, Rosie Dickens (Usborne Publishing, 2005)

More paintings to see

Poplars, Claude Monet, The Fitzwilliam Museum, Cambridge

Rouen Cathedral Façade, Claude Monet, National Museum of Wales, Cardiff

The Water Lily Pond, Claude Monet, National Gallery, London

Index